Contents

YOUR LUNGS

Try to sit perfectly still. Notice how your chest rises and falls? That is because your lungs are working to keep you breathing. Breathing is **involuntary**. Your lungs do it without your thinking about it.

Lungs are baglike organs, or body parts. All animals that have a backbone and breathe air (like you!) have lungs. When an animal inhales (breathes in), air filled with

Breathing is an example of an involuntary action. Without the body's involuntary actions, other actions like standing, smiling, and taking a picture would be impossible.

LET'S FIND OUT! THE HUMAN BODY

THE LUNGS IN YOUR BODY

CHRISTINE FIGORITO

Britannica Educational Publishing

IN ASSOCIATION WITH

ROSEN EDUCATIONAL SERVICES

Published in 2015 by Britannica Educational Publishing (a trademark of Encyclopædia Britannica, Inc.) in association with The Rosen Publishing Group, Inc.
29 East 21st Street, New York, NY 10010

Distributed exclusively by Rosen Publishing.
To see additional Britannica Educational Publishing titles, go to rosenpublishing.com.

First Edition

Britannica Educational Publishing
J. E. Luebering: Director, Core Reference Group
Mary Rose McCudden: Editor, Britannica Student Encyclopedia

Rosen Publishing
Hope Lourie Killcoyne: Executive Editor
Isobel Towne: Editor
Nelson Sá: Art Director
Michael Moy: Designer
Cindy Reiman: Photography Manager

Library of Congress Cataloging-in-Publication Data

Figorito, Christine, 1971– author.
The lungs in your body/Christine Figorito.—First edition.
pages cm.—(Let's find out! The human body)
Includes bibliographical references and index.
ISBN 978-1-62275-628-5 (library bound)—ISBN 978-1-62275-629-2 (pbk.)—
ISBN 978-1-62275-630-8 (6-pack)
1. Lungs—Juvenile literature. 2. Respiration—Juvenile literature. I. Title.
QP121.F54 2015
612.2'4—dc23

2014013910

Manufactured in the United States of America

Photo credits: Cover racorn/Shutterstock.com; cover (background), pp. 1, 5, interior pages background Sebastian Kaulitzki/Shutterstock.com; pp. 4, 24 bikeriderlondon/Shutterstock.com; p. 6 dotshock/Shutterstock.com; pp. 7, 10, 20, 27 Encyclopædia Britannica, Inc.; p. 8 BSIP/Science Source; p. 9 absolutimages/Shutterstock.com; p. 11 Fuse/Thinkstock; p. 12 Margot Petrowski/Shutterstock.com; p. 13 mandygodbehear/iStock/Thinkstock: p 14 Cat Longon/E+/Getty Images; p. 15 Eye of Science/Science Source; p. 16 Springer Medizin/Science Photo Library/Getty Images; p. 17 Biophoto Associates/Photo Researchers/Getty Images; p. 18 Michel Gilles/Science Source; p. 19 Tim Platt/Iconica/Getty Images; p. 21 Alila Medical Media/Shutterstock.com; p. 22 M Phillips David/Science Source/Getty Images; p. 23 Hero Images/Getty Images; p. 25 SPL/Science Source; p. 26 Steven Reisman/Moment Select/Getty Images; p. 28 oliveromg/Shutterstock.com; p. 29 iofoto/Shutterstock.com.

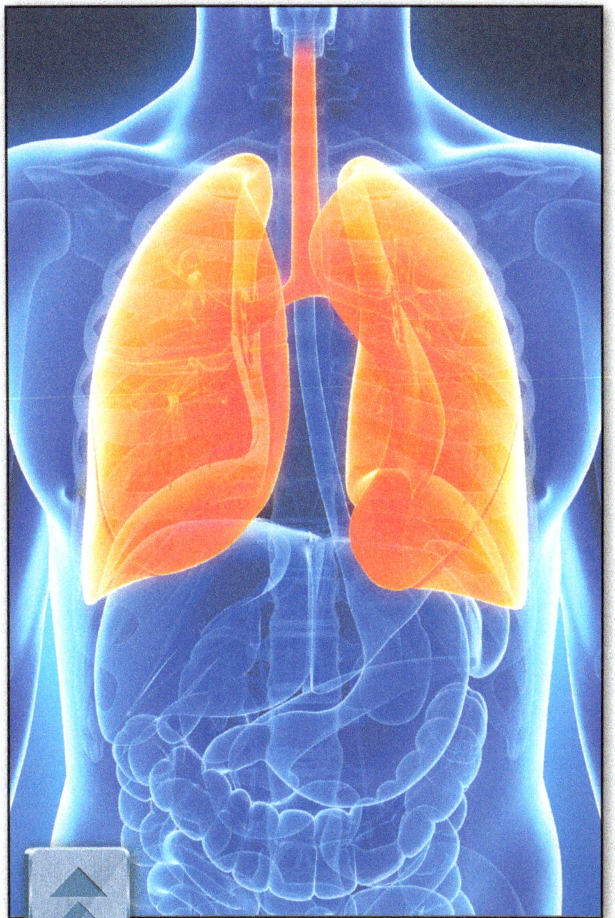

The left lung is smaller than the right lung. This makes room for the heart to fit in between them.

oxygen flows into the lungs. The body needs a steady supply of oxygen to live. When an animal exhales (breathes out), a different gas flows out of the lungs.

Other organs in the body help with breathing. For example, the brain sends signals to the lungs to make sure the breathing never stops.

Involuntary means not done on purpose. Breathing is an involuntary action because the body does it automatically.

Locating the Lungs

A human body has two lungs. One lung is on each side of the chest. They make one of the largest organs in the body. Each lung has about 300 million tiny air sacs. If it were possible to stretch these air sacs out and lay them flat,your lungs would cover an area as large as a tennis court! The left lung is a little smaller than the right lung. Its smaller size makes room for

If spread out, an adult lung can cover half the area of a tennis court. That's a lot of lung!

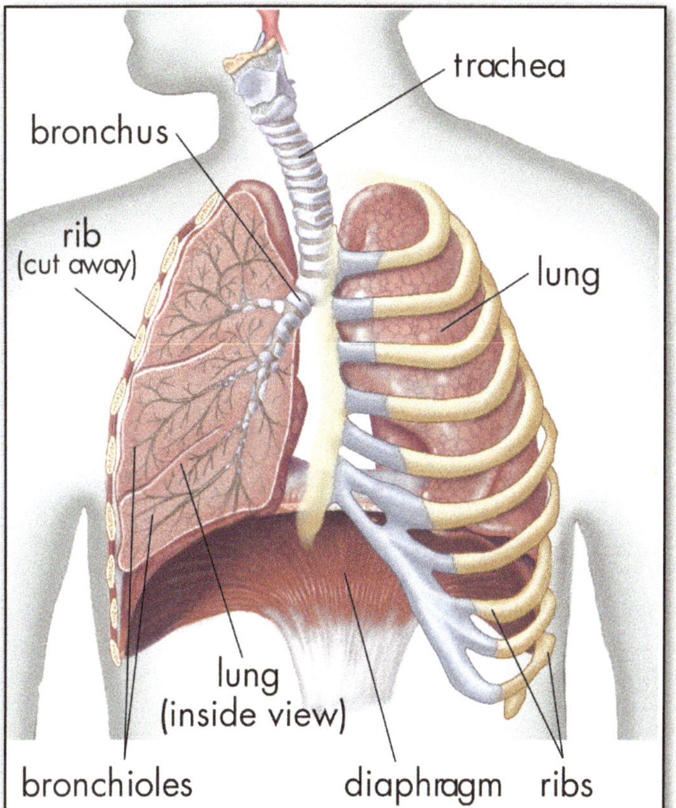

Ribs protect both lungs. The diagram shows the inside of one lung, with the ribs cut away.

the heart, which sits between them. The lungs are protected by the rib cage, which surrounds them. The lungs sit on a muscle called a diaphragm. In normal breathing the diaphragm and muscles between the ribs automatically tighten and relax. This movement helps the lungs to fill with air and to empty.

Compare and Contrast

How do different parts of the body help the lungs?

The Respiratory System

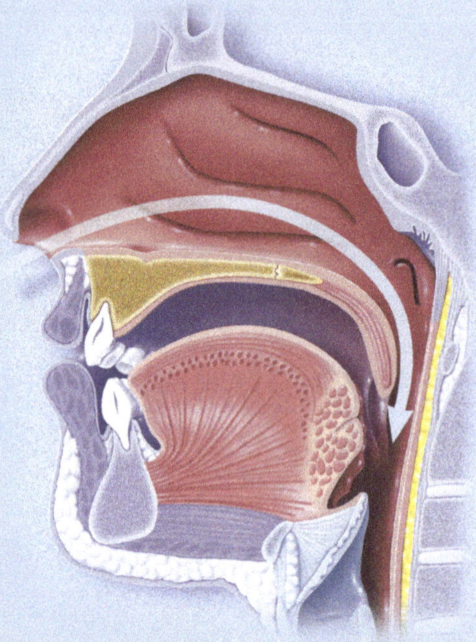

This diagram shows the inside of the nasal cavity and the mouth. Air enters the body through the nose (as shown by the arrow) and the mouth.

Lungs do not breathe by themselves. A body's breathing relies on its entire respiratory system. The human respiratory system includes a number of parts: mouth, nose, throat, voice box, windpipe, bronchial tubes, and lungs.

Air enters the respiratory system through the nose or mouth. The throat has two passageways: one for air and one for food. The passage for food is called the esophagus, which is part of the digestive system. The upper part of the air passage contains the voice box. The lower part contains the windpipe. The windpipe separates into two main branches called bronchial tubes, or bronchi. Each attaches to a lung.

Think About It

How can coughing help someone who has accidentally breathed liquid into his or her windpipe?

People cough when something irritates, or bothers, the respiratory system. This can happen when food or liquid goes down the windpipe instead of the esophagus when someone is eating.

Oxygen Provider

The main role of the lungs is to provide the body with oxygen. Oxygen is a gas that the body needs in order to survive. The lungs also allow the body to get rid of another gas, called carbon dioxide.

When you breathe in, air enters the lungs. Tiny blood vessels within the lungs **absorb** oxygen from the

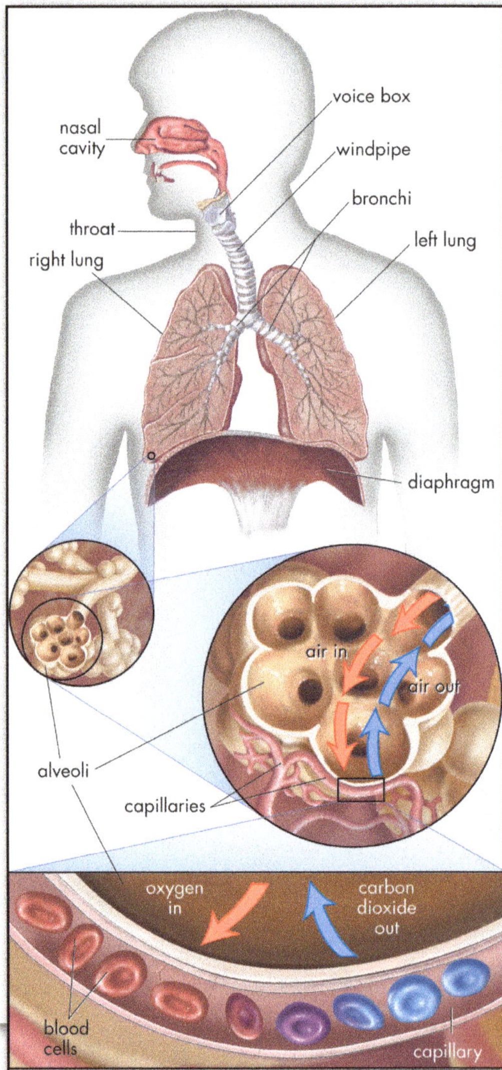

Tiny alveoli and capillaries in the lungs exchange oxygen for carbon dioxide.

air. The blood then carries the oxygen through other blood vessels to all the cells of the body. Cells are basic units that make up all living things. The cells take in the oxygen and release carbon dioxide back into the blood. The blood brings the carbon dioxide to the lungs, where it is released when you breathe out.

Absorb means to take in. A sponge absorbs water. When it's squeezed, the water is released.

While this girl is blowing up her balloon, she is getting rid of carbon dioxide, which is released from her body every time she exhales.

Let's Talk

This girl's vocal cords are open when she breathes in. When she talks, the cords come together, making a smaller space that vibrates when the air passes through.

You also need your lungs in order to talk. Your voice box sits at the top of the windpipe. Inside the voice box are vocal cords. These are a pair of stretchy folds that create the voice. As air exhales from your lungs, it passes between the vocal cords and makes them vibrate. This vibration makes sounds. Your voice box makes these sounds louder. Then they pass through your throat, mouth, and nose.

To **vibrate** is to move quickly back and forth. Can you think of something that vibrates?

You use your tongue, teeth, lips, jaw, and palate (roof of the mouth) to shape the sounds to make words. If you want to say many words quickly or speak loudly, you need to exhale more air. Shouting requires a lot of air from the lungs!

To shout, this boy has to take a deep breath. He can also make his voice deeper or higher by tightening and relaxing his vocal cords.

PROTECTION

Another job of the lungs is to help keep germs and other harmful things out of the body. Inside the lungs are cells that produce mucus. Mucus is a sticky substance that traps pollutants and bacteria. Tiny hairs called cilia also keep dirt and bacteria out of the lungs. They move in waves to push the mucus up out of

Coughing helps move mucus and bacteria out of the body.

Bacteria are single-celled living things found in all natural environments. Some bacteria can cause illness.

the airways. When you cough, the mucus as well as the bacteria and other irritating particles are forced out of the body. The lungs also have patrolling cells that "swallow up" foreign particles or destroy them.

This is a picture of the inside lining of a lung under a microscope. The cilia on top move back and forth to push dirt out.

What Lungs Look Like

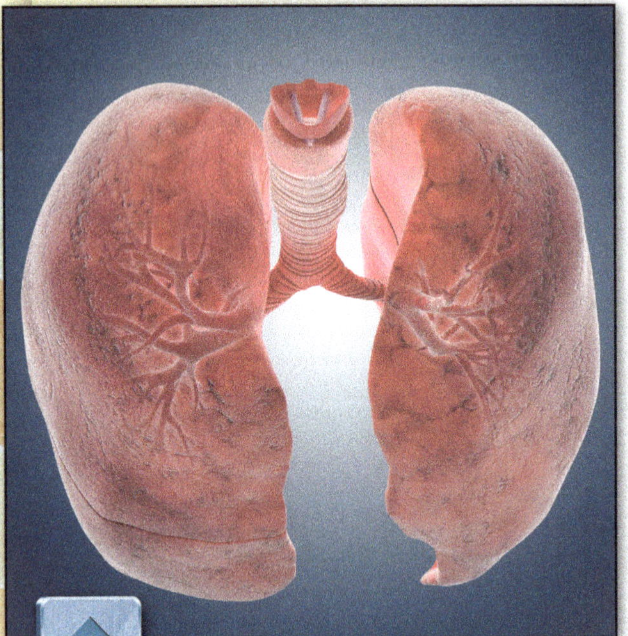

Healthy lungs, like these, are pink and feel spongy. Unhealthy lungs are gray or black and are smaller than healthy lungs.

Healthy lungs look pink on the outside and feel spongy. The right lung has three rounded sections called lobes. The left lung has two lobes.

Tubes used for carrying air connect to the lungs in a branchlike manner. The series begins with the windpipe. Before it enters the lungs, it branches into the two tubes called bronchi.

Think About It

What other parts of the body branch out from one large part into smaller parts?

Each of these leads to a different lung. The bronchial tubes then divide into a web of smaller tubes called bronchioles. There are about 30,000 bronchioles in just one lung. Each bronchiole leads to many tiny air sacs, called alveoli. The air sacs are what make a lung feel spongy.

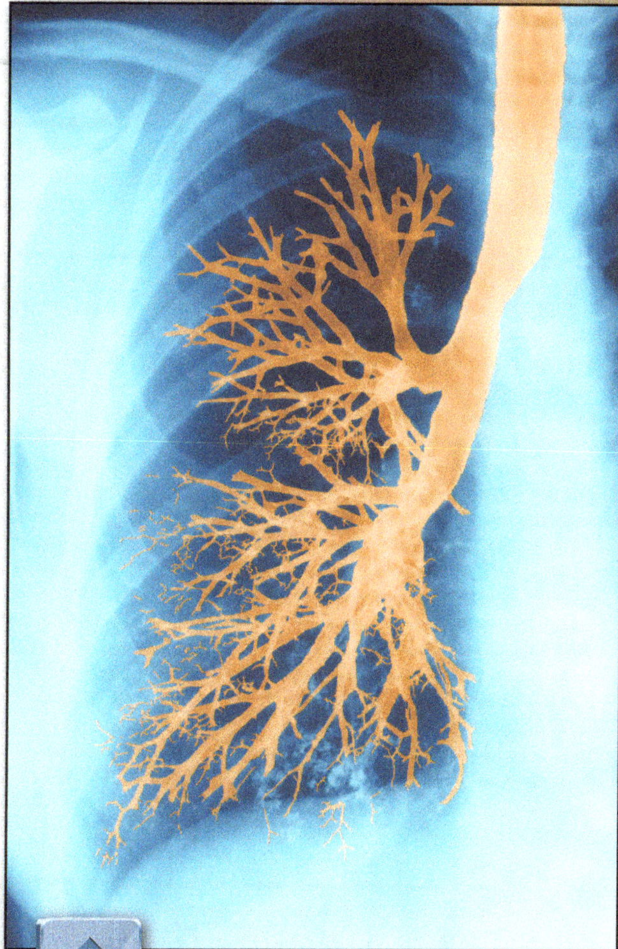

This image shows one of the bronchi and the bronchioles, which are the smallest branches in the lungs. They're less than one millimeter wide.

Every Tiny Part Has a Big Job

The alveoli, the tiny air sacs in the lungs, are covered with blood vessels called capillaries. These capillaries are so small that blood cells must line up one by one to get through them! Although tiny,

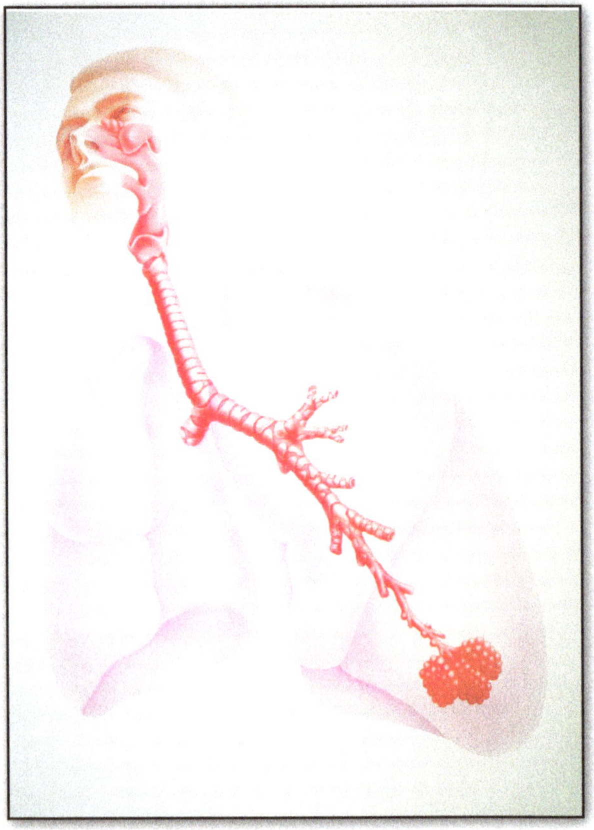

The alveoli are air sacs located at the end of the bronchioles. They look like tiny clusters of grapes.

Think About It

When people are scared, does more air than normal go into their lungs? Why or why not?

alveoli and capillaries are important. Through them, oxygen gets to the blood cells. The blood cells then deliver the oxygen to your entire body.

If people are afraid or worried, they can breathe up to 100 times per minute.

Inhale (Breathe In)

Breathing in is called inhaling. When the muscle at the base of the lungs, called the diaphragm, moves down and the ribs move out, the area inside your chest grows larger. Air then flows in through your mouth or nose, down the windpipe, and into your lungs.

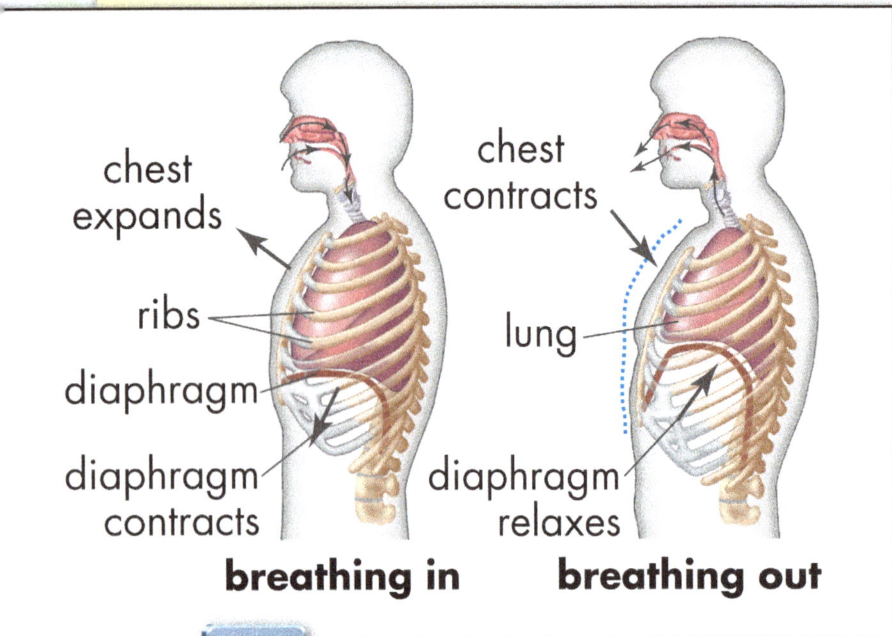

Oxygen gas in the air is able to pass through

The diaphragm contracts and relaxes, forcing air into and out of the lungs.

the thin walls of the alveoli into the capillaries. Red blood cells inside the capillaries pick up the oxygen and take it to the heart. Then the heart sends the blood filled with oxygen to all the cells in your body.

COMPARE AND CONTRAST

Why might you take short, quick breaths rather than long, deep ones?

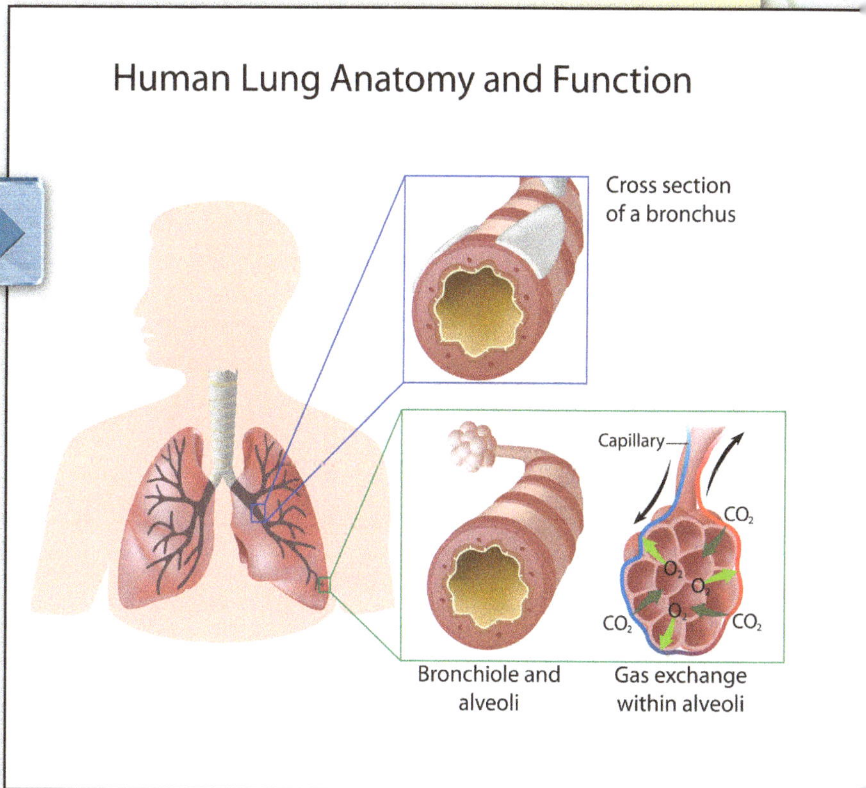

This diagram shows the inside of a bronchus, bronchiole, and alveoli. In the alveoli, the blood cells pick up and drop off oxygen (O) and carbon dioxide (CO_2).

Exhale (Breathe Out)

After you inhale, you must exhale, or breathe out. Exhaling is important for ridding the body of waste gas. As red blood cells deliver oxygen to the body's cells, they pick up waste gas that the cells do not need. These waste gases include carbon dioxide and water vapor.

The red blood cells carry the waste gas back

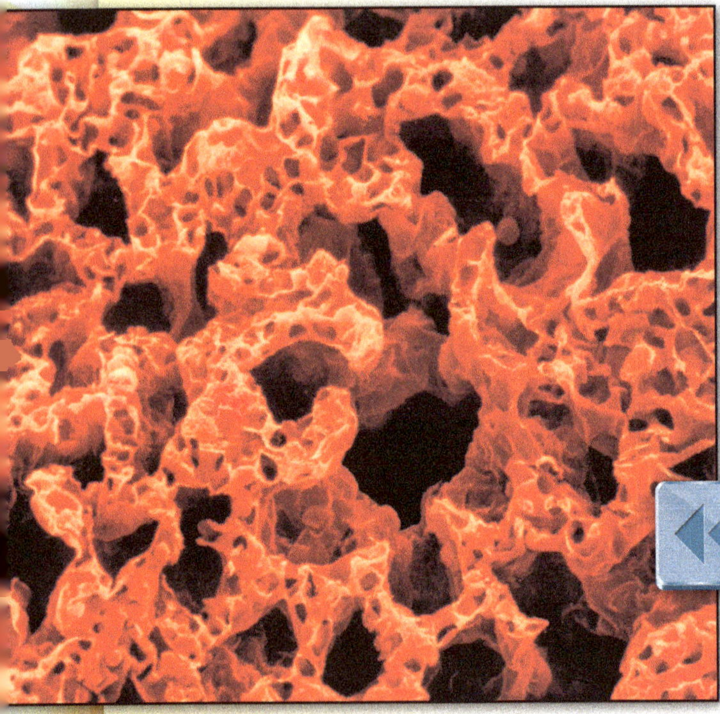

Alveoli in the lungs are pictured here. The alveoli are grouped together like interlinked caves. They are not separate and individual sacs.

to the lungs. They travel through the capillaries and send the waste gas into the alveoli. The diaphragm muscle then pushes the waste gas through the bronchioles, out the bronchi, up the windpipe, and finally out the nose or mouth.

THINK ABOUT IT
Why do slow, deep breaths relax the body?

Even on a cold day, air that is exhaled will be warm. This is because air picks up heat as it travels through the body.

You can see your breath on a cold day because the air you exhale picks up heat as it moves through your body.

WHY LUNGS GET SICK

Lungs can develop many different problems. Some people have a breathing problem called asthma. Their bronchioles sometimes tighten so that air cannot get into the alveoli. It is one of the most common long-term health problems in children.

During asthma attacks, bronchial tubes swell, making it hard to breathe. An inhaler has medicine that opens the tubes, letting air flow easily into and out of the lungs.

Another sickness is bronchitis, which is when the bronchi are sore or damaged. Bronchitis makes it hard for air to get to the alveoli. People with bronchitis cannot breathe easily, cough a lot, and feel pain in their chests.

Think About It

Some people live with one lung, after a sick lung has been removed. What might they need to be mindful of with just one lung?

An illness called pneumonia causes the lungs to swell. The lungs have a hard time absorbing the oxygen in the air. Pneumonia makes people feel very sick and tired.

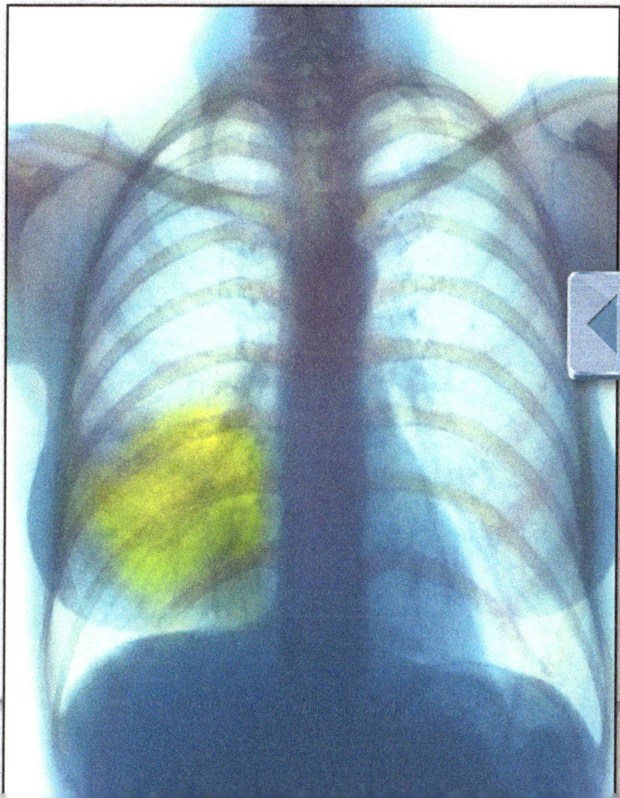

This X-ray shows lungs with pneumonia. The alveoli are filled with fluid and air can't pass through them. You can see the fluid in the yellow spot in the right lung.

Thank You for Not Smoking

Smoke from fires can be as dangerous as the flames. If the smoke is inhaled, it can seriously damage the lungs.

Smoking is bad for the whole body. It is especially bad for the lungs! Smoke damages cilia so that they cannot keep dirt and other harmful things out of the lungs. Smoke also breaks down the walls of the alveoli.

Over time, inhaling cigarette smoke causes the lungs to become so damaged that

Think About It

How do firefighters keep themselves from inhaling smoke?

they are unable to heal. Emphysema or lung cancer can result. Both are deadly diseases of the lungs.

People who inhale smoke in the air from other people's smoking can also get these diseases.

In many ways, the lungs are strong. However, any kind of smoke can easily damage them. Firefighters often warn that more people die from inhaling the smoke of a fire than from burn injuries.

An illustration shows how lungs are affected by emphysema. The disease causes the walls of the alveoli to break down, reducing the efficiency of the lungs.

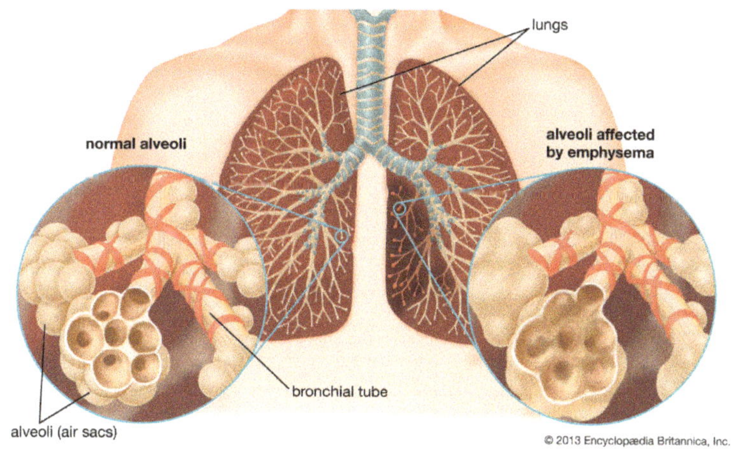

Keeping Your Lungs Healthy

What do your lungs help you do every day? They do more than help you breathe, talk, or shout. One could argue that the lungs help the entire body do everything that it does. That is why it is important to keep your lungs healthy!

You can help your lungs stay healthy by not smoking. Other pollution in the air, such as exhaust from cars, can also hurt the lungs.

Exercising is a good way to keep your lungs strong and healthy. It is good for your whole body, too. When you exercise, your body has to

It's important to keep your lungs healthy so that you can breathe, run, laugh, and much more!

THINK ABOUT IT

Think of different times when your lungs were working hard. What were you doing?

do more than it usually does. For example, running requires your legs to move faster. Your body cells need more oxygen to do that extra work. You must breathe harder and faster to get oxygen to your cells. That exercises your lungs, which makes them stronger and healthier.

When you exercise, blood flow to the alveoli increases, getting more oxygen into the blood. The lungs absorb the extra oxygen and the blood sends it to the muscles.

Glossary

alveoli Tiny air sacs at the end of each bronchiole.

asthma A physical condition that makes it hard for the lungs to breathe.

blood vessels Small tubes that carry blood to different parts of the body.

bronchi The two tubes that lead from the windpipe into each lung; a single tube is called a bronchus.

bronchioles Small branches of the bronchus.

bronchitis An illness in which the bronchial tubes become sore or damaged and coughing results.

capillaries The smallest tubes that carry blood through the body.

carbon dioxide A colorless waste gas that is made when people breathe.

cell A very small, basic unit of all living things.

diaphragm A dome-shaped sheet of muscle under the lungs that is used for breathing.

emphysema A serious disease of the lungs that is often caused by smoking.

mucus A thick liquid that is made in some parts of the body for protection.

organ A part of the body that has a specific job to do.

oxygen A gas found in air that is needed by most life-forms on Earth to live.

pneumonia A serious illness that affects the lungs and makes it hard to breathe.

respiratory system A group of organs and tissues that work together to help the body breathe.

rib cage The bony frame that protects organs that are located in the chest.

tissue A family of cells that live close together and work together to do the same job.

vocal cords Thin pieces of folded tissue that help the voice make sounds.

voice box Part of the throat that holds the vocal cords; also called the larynx.

windpipe A long tube from the neck to the chest that carries air in and out of the lungs; also called the trachea.

For More Information

Books

Calderwood, Wendy. *Kirby Kids: Into the Lungs.* Mustang, OK: Tate Publishing, 2012.

Caster, Shannon. *Lungs*. New York, NY: Rosen Publishing, 2010.

Shea, John. *The Respiratory System.* New York, NY: Gareth Stevens Publishing, 2012.

Williams, Ben. *Look Inside: Your Heart and Lungs.* Huntington Beach, CA: Teacher Created Materials Publishing, 2011.

Websites

Because of the changing nature of Internet links, Rosen Publishing has developed an online list of websites related to the subject of this book. This site is updated regularly. Please use this link to access the list:

http://www.rosenlinks.com/LFO/Lungs

INDEX